WHO LOVES A GARDEN
STILL HIS EDEN KEEPS

A.B.ALCOTT

She Who Loves a Garden

Illustrated by
Mary Engelbreit

Andrews and McMeel
A Universal Press Syndicate Company
Kansas City

is a registered trademark of Mary Engelbreit Enterprises, Inc.

10 9 8 7 6 5 4 3

ISBN: 0-8362-4612-8

She Who Loves
a Garden

She who loves a garden
loves the wonders of creation
and appreciates the joy
that flowers bring.

JUST LIVING IS NOT ENOUGH... ONE MUST HAVE SUNSHINE, FREEDOM, AND A LITTLE FLOWER

·HANS CHRISTIAN ANDERSEN·

She who loves a garden
likes to make the earth more lovely
and enjoys the beauty
she's contributing.

She who loves a garden
has a reverence
for all creatures . . .

THE SIMPLE NEWS
THAT NATURE TOLD,
WITH TENDER MAJESTY

EMILY DICKINSON

. . . from endangered whales
cavorting in the seas . . .

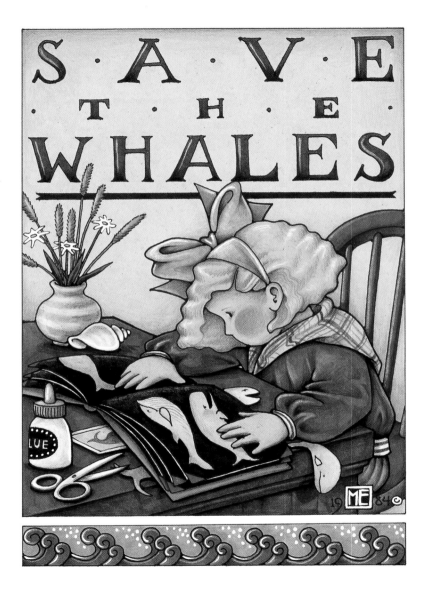

. . . to the warm and furry friends
that make their home
within the forests . . .

Dear

. . . and the songbirds
nesting high within the trees.

MAKE A NEST of PLEASANT THOUGHTS.

JOHN RUSKIN

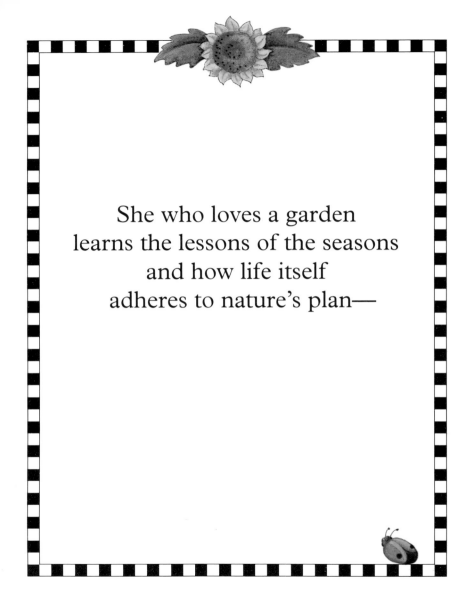

She who loves a garden
learns the lessons of the seasons
and how life itself
adheres to nature's plan—

SILENTLY, ONE BY ONE IN THE INFINITE MEADOWS of HEAVEN, BLOSSOMED THE LOVELY·STARS, THE FORGET·ME·NOTS of ANGELS

—LONGFELLOW—

that from every winter sleep
there comes a wonderful awakening
holding promise as it has
since time began.

She who loves a garden
knows it's only hers to borrow—

that the tender care
she puts into the soil . . .

COME FORTH
INTO THE LIGHT
of THINGS,
LET NATURE
BE YOUR TEACHER
WILLIAM WORDSWORTH

. . . helps the children of tomorrow
carry on what she has started,
giving strength and
lasting value to her toil.

She who loves a garden
loves the joys of simple living
and the peace on which
no man can put a price.

She who loves a garden
has a very special treasure . . .
for she has found
her private paradise.